JOEL C. ROSENBERG

EPICENTER
STUDY GUIDE

TYNDALE HOUSE PUBLISHERS, INC., CAROL STREAM, ILLINOIS

Visit Tyndale's exciting Web site at www.tyndale.com

TYNDALE and Tyndale's quill logo are registered trademarks of Tyndale House Publishers, Inc.

Epicenter Study Guide

Study questions developed by Jennifer Lamont Leo.

Designed by Dean H. Renninger.

Quoted excerpts are taken from *Epicenter*, © 2006 by Joel C. Rosenberg. Used by permission.

Unless otherwise indicated, all Scripture quotations are taken from the *New American Standard Bible*®, copyright © 1960, 1962, 1963, 1968, 1971, 1972, 1973, 1975, 1977, 1995 by The Lockman Foundation. Used by permission.

Scripture quotations marked KJV are taken from the *Holy Bible*, King James Version.

ISBN-10: 1-4143-2154-6

ISBN-13: 978-1-4143-2154-7

Printed in the United States of America

14 13 12 11 10 09 08
 7   6   5   4   3   2   1

TABLE OF CONTENTS

v // WELCOME TO THE EPICENTER

ix // INTRODUCTION: ALL EYES ON THE EPICENTER

1 // UNDERSTANDING GOD'S HEART FOR THE EPICENTER

5 // Chapter 1: Predicting the Future

8 // Chapter 2: The Genesis of Jihad

11 // Chapter 3: Connecting the Dots

15 // SETTING THE STAGE: PART I

20 // Chapter 4: The Third Lens

23 // Chapter 5: Future Headline: Israel Discovers Massive Reserves
of Oil, Gas

25 // Chapter 6: Future Headline: Treaties and Truces Leave Israelis
More Secure than Ever Before

27 // SETTING THE STAGE: PART II

31 // Chapter 7: Future Headline: A Czar Rises in Russia, Raising Fears
of a New Cold War

35 // Chapter 8: Future Headline: Kremlin Joins "Axis of Evil," Forms Military
Alliance with Iran

38 // Chapter 9: Future Headline: Moscow Extends Military Alliance to Include
Arab, Islamic World

41 // **USING THE THIRD LENS: PART I**

49 // **Chapter 10: Future Headline: Global Tensions Soar as Russia Targets Israel**

52 // **Chapter 11: Future Headline: New War Erupts in Middle East as Earthquakes, Pandemics Hit Europe, Africa, Asia**

56 // **Chapter 12: Future Headline: Iraq Emerges from Chaos as Region's Wealthiest Country**

59 // **USING THE THIRD LENS: PART II**

66 // **Chapter 13: Future Headline: Jews Build Third Temple in Jerusalem**

69 // **Chapter 14: Future Headline: Muslims Turn to Christ in Record Numbers**

73 // **Chapter 15: Tracking the Tremors**

81 // CLOSING PERSONAL NOTE

83 // PRAYER JOURNAL

85 // APPENDIX: BIBLE PROPHECY AND YOUR SPIRITUAL JOURNEY

89 // ACKNOWLEDGMENTS

91 // SUGGESTED READING

WELCOME TO THE EPICENTER

Wars and rumors of war. Jihadists in Jerusalem. Chaos in Gaza. Missiles in Lebanon. Suicide bombers in Iraq. Genocide in Sudan. An Iranian president vowing to wipe Israel "off the map." Millions convinced the Messiah is coming. Poverty. Illiteracy. Hardship and suffering. Yet always a fervent prayer for peace.

No wonder the eyes of the nations are riveted on Israel and her Islamic neighbors, the epicenter of the momentous events that are shaking our world and shaping our future.

What will tomorrow bring? How will the rumblings in the Middle East affect your world and change your future? Does the Bible actually give us advance intelligence as to what is coming, what it means, and how we can be ready?

WHY USE THIS STUDY GUIDE?

As you embark on a journey to find the answers to these important and increasingly urgent questions, I hope that you will find this *Epicenter Study Guide* helpful. I wrote it for several reasons:

1. To help readers of my nonfiction book *Epicenter* continue and even accelerate their own personal quest to understand the Middle East's past, present, and future.

2. To help pastors and other religious leaders better explain God's plans for the people of the epicenter.

3. To create a resource that would encourage small group studies and discussions of the epicenter.

4. To inspire a new generation of evangelical Christians with a passion for compassion, a burning desire to bless Israel and her neighbors in real and practical ways.

5. To mobilize a global movement of millions of people praying daily, knowledgeably, and faithfully for the peace of Jerusalem and the entire region, according to Psalm 122:6.

What are your goals for reading using this guide? What do you hope to learn? to achieve? Knowledge is important. So is faith. But the Bible says, "faith without works is dead" (James 2:26). I agree. For me, it's not enough to know the history and future of the Middle East. Nor is it enough simply to believe that God loves all the people of the Middle East—Jew and Gentile alike—and has a wonderful plan and purpose for their lives. For me the question is, so what? How will you and I act on that knowledge? How will our knowledge and our faith spur us to love and good deeds? How will what we know and what we believe change us? How will it shape what we are willing to say and what we are willing to do? These are the questions that matter most.

If you aren't open to having your life change radically, I would recommend you skip this study altogether. But if you are truly serious about pursuing truth and truly open to letting God take you on an adventure more exciting that you could have hoped for, dreamed of, or imagined, then by all means, please proceed.

HOW TO USE THIS STUDY GUIDE

Along with study questions for every chapter of *Epicenter*, this guide includes five additional studies with new material that will help you explore what the Scriptures say about the epicenter. As you begin, a few quick thoughts.

First, I recommend that you carve out at least thirty minutes a day, preferably in the morning, for at least five days a week to work on the questions in this guide, read the Scriptures that I cite, chew them over, and have some time for prayer. This will help you get the most out of the material and help you establish the wise habit of a daily appointment with the living God, if you don't have such an appointment already.

Second, in addition to studying through this material on your own, I recommend that you find a friend or a group of friends and meet together once a week over a cup of coffee to compare notes, discuss what you're learning, and pray together. Proverbs 27:17 tells us that just as "iron sharpens iron, so one man sharpens another." You may not always agree with the views and perspectives others have on this material, but you will more than likely think deeper and more carefully if you don't study in isolation. Plus, you'll have more fun and hopefully develop stronger friendships along the way.

Third, I recommend that you use a New American Standard Bible (NASB) to answer the questions in this guide. There are many excellent translations of the Bible available, to be sure, and you would be wise to cross-check passages with the NASB *and* other translations. But I have found that studying Bible prophecy requires as precise a word-for-word translation from the Hebrew and Greek as you can possibly get. My experience, along with conversations with Bible scholars and Hebrew and Greek experts, has led me to trust the NASB the most for my own personal study of prophecy.

That said, *"I pray that the eyes of your heart may be enlightened, so that you will know what is the hope of His calling, what are the riches of the glory of His inheritance in the saints, and what is the surpassing greatness of His power toward us who believe"* (Ephesians 1:18-19). May God bless you as you begin your journey.

Joel C. Rosenberg
JERUSALEM, ISRAEL
JANUARY 2008

INTRODUCTION:
ALL EYES ON THE EPICENTER

"Like it or not, we live in interesting times."
// *EPICENTER,* PAGE xix

1. As you begin reading *Epicenter*, how extensively have you been following the events unfolding around the world? Are you an avid watcher of the evening news? Or have places like the Middle East seemed too remote to be very concerned about?

   _____

   _____

   _____

   _____

   _____

2. Do you know someone currently serving in the armed forces in the Middle East or who has served there in the past? Have you

been tracking developments in Israel or the Muslim world more closely since the events of September 11, 2001?

_____

_____

_____

_____

3. Pick up a current newspaper or newsmagazine—or go to an online news source—and jot down some of the headlines concerning Jerusalem, Israel, and the Middle East. Why do you think so much attention is focused on this part of the world? Is too much attention being paid, in your view, or not enough?

_____

_____

_____

_____

4. Do you think it's important for Christians to keep a close watch on world events? Why or why not?

_____

_____

_____

_____

5. Read Matthew 10:16. What does it mean to be "shrewd as serpents"? How might this command of Jesus relate to staying informed about what's going on around the world?

_____

_____

_____

_____

6. Are you new to reading or studying the Bible and learning about the epicenter from God's perspective? If so, what got you interested in this study? If you have been studying the Bible for some time, why did you choose this particular study at this particular time?

_____

_____

_____

_____

7. The _Random House Unabridged Dictionary_ defines _epicenter_ in two ways: as a geological term describing "a point, directly above the true center of disturbance, from which the shock waves of an earthquake apparently radiate"; or as "a focal point, as of activity." In your view, is the term _epicenter_ an apt description for the Middle East today? Why or why not?

_____

_____

_____

8. Current events are not the only reason to describe Israel and her neighbors as the "epicenter." Look up the following passages of Scripture. What is the Bible's perspective of this part of the world?

EZEKIEL 5:5 • EZEKIEL 38:12 • ACTS 1:6-8

_____

_____

_____

_____

9. What can you conclude from these verses about how the God of the Bible regards Israel and Jerusalem?

_____

_____

_____

_____

10. Look up Psalm 122 and study it closely. According to these verses of Scripture, how are we supposed to regard Israel and Jerusalem?

_____

_____

_____

_____

11. What threats to Jerusalem are currently being reported in the media? What are some specific ways, therefore, you can "pray for

the peace of Jerusalem"? Jot down some thoughts and then take a few minutes to lift up these needs before your Father in heaven.

_____

_____

_____

_____

GREENLAND

GREENLAND SEA

Denmark Strait

AR

Reykjavik ● ICELAND

NORWEGIAN

SEA

ATLANTIC

NORWAY

Oslo ●

S

SCOTLAND

OCEAN

NORTH

Skagerrak

Göt ●

● Edinburgh

● Belfast

SEA

DENMARK

IRELAND

Copenhagen ●

Dublin ●

ENGLAND

WALES

NETHERLANDS

Cardiff ●

London ●

● The Hague

Berlin ●

BELGIUM ● Brussels

GERMANY

Paris ● Luxembourg

LUXEMBOURG

CZEC

FRANCE

Vien

Bay of
Biscay

SWITZERLAND

● Bern

AUSTR

Bilbao ●

Ljubljana

SLOVENIA

Porto ●

Monaco ●

San Marino ●

HE

Andorra la Vella

PORTUGAL

Madrid ●

ANDORRA

ITALY

Lisbon ●

● Barcelona

● Rome

S P A I N

● Sevilla

M
E
D
I
T
E
R
R
A
N

● Malaga

Strait of Gibraltar

Gibraltar

Algiers ●

Casablanca ● ● Rabat

Tunis ●

Marrakech ●

MOROCCO

MALTA

Las Palmas ●

TUNISIA

El Aaiun ●

Tripoli ●

WESTERN
SAHARA

A L G E R I A

L I

MAURITANIA

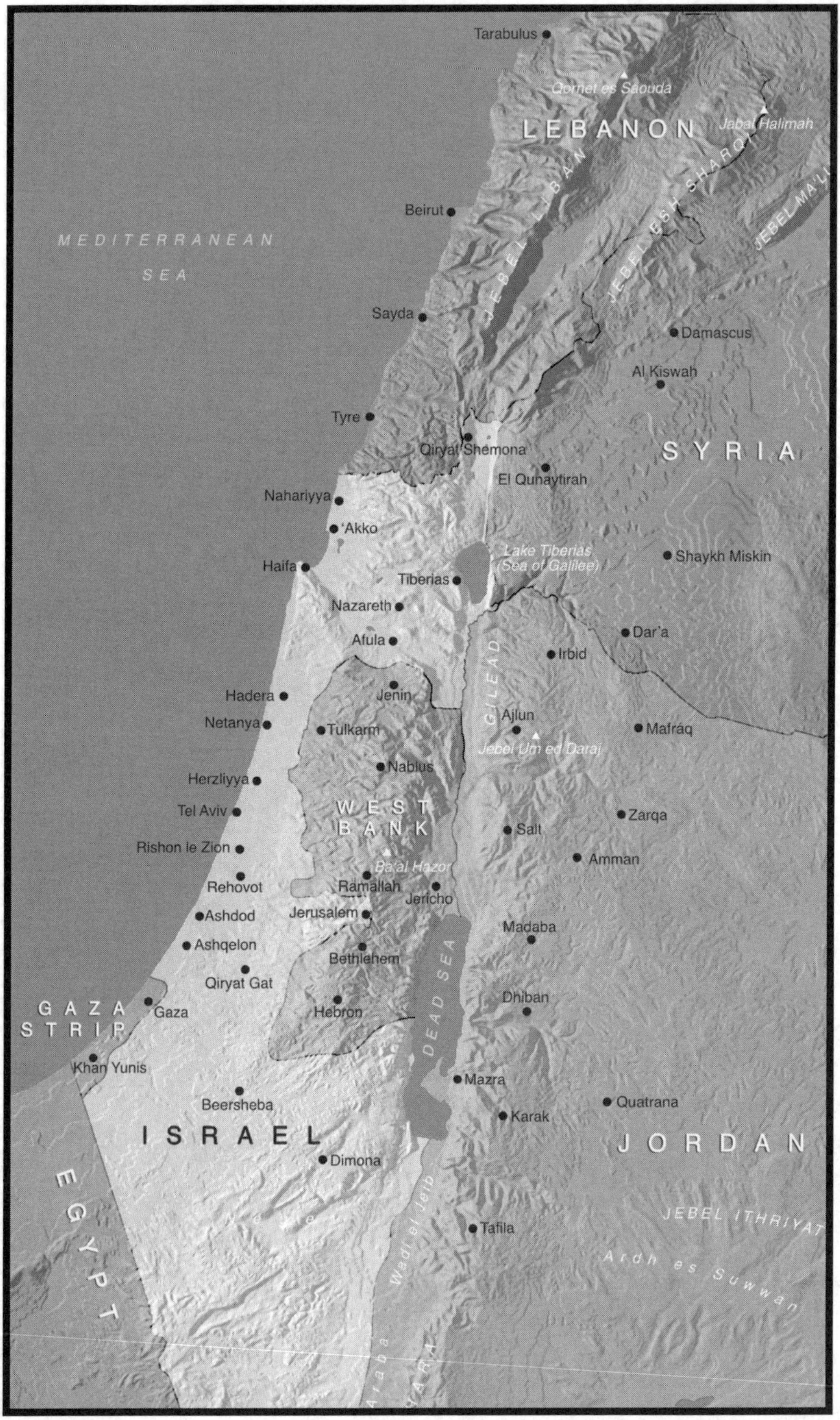

Tarabulus
Qornet es Saouda
LEBANON
Jabal Halimah
JEBEL LIBAN
JEBEL ESH SHARQI
Beirut
MEDITERRANEAN
SEA
Sayda
Damascus
Al Kiswah
Tyre
Qiryat Shemona
SYRIA
El Qunaytirah
Nahariyya
'Akko
Lake Tiberias
(Sea of Galilee)
Shaykh Miskin
Haifa
Tiberias
Nazareth
Dar'a
Afula
Irbid
GILEAD
Hadera
Jenin
Netanya
Ajlun
Mafráq
Tulkarm
Jebel Um ed Daraj
Nablus
Herzliyya
Tel Aviv
WEST
BANK
Zarqa
Salt
Rishon le Zion
Amman
Ba'al Hazor
Rehovot
Ramallah
Jericho
Ashdod
Jerusalem
Madaba
Ashqelon
Bethlehem
DEAD SEA
Qiryat Gat
GAZA
STRIP
Gaza
Hebron
Dhiban
Khan Yunis
Mazra
Beersheba
Quatrana
Karak
ISRAEL
JORDAN
Dimona
EGYPT
JEBEL ITHRIYAT
Tafila
Wadi el Jeib
Ardh es Suwwan

UNDERSTANDING GOD'S HEART FOR THE EPICENTER

While the Bible is God's love letter and instruction manual for *all* of mankind, it was written in the epicenter, through people living in the epicenter, and it teaches us much about the history—and future—of the epicenter. The narrative of the Bible even begins in the epicenter. The Garden of Eden, described in Genesis chapters 2 and 3, is widely believed by scholars to have been located in the country we now call Iraq. The flood described in Genesis chapters 6 through 8 began in the Middle East and eventually covered the entire earth. Genesis 8:4 says Noah's ark "rested upon the mountains of Ararat." Some scholars believe that mountain range is in northeastern Turkey or northwestern Iran. In order to properly understand current and future events in the epicenter, it's important to have a solid grasp of its history.

1. One of the most important early passages of Scripture as it relates to prophecy is Genesis chapter 10. Take a moment to read it now. Then read Ezekiel 38:1-6. Which names do you read in these verses that are also found in Genesis 10:2. Read Genesis 11:1-9. What modern-day country was known as Babel or Babylon back

in the time Genesis was written? After God chose to confuse the languages of the people groups centered around Babel, what did he also choose to do with these nations?

_____

_____

_____

2. Later in this study, we will track where these descendants of Noah migrated to, where they eventually settled, and what modern-day countries describe where these people groups are located. For now, though, let's focus on the journey of one of the families scattered by God after the incident in Babel. Read Genesis 11:27-31 and consider Abram's family, which eventually became the nation of Israel. Who was Abram's father? What city or village does the text say their family lived in (in the country we now call Iraq)?

_____

_____

_____

_____

3. Read Genesis 12:1-5. Why did Abram set out for Canaan? What did God promise him? How did God say he would treat those who blessed Abram and his descendants? How did God say he would treat those who cursed Abram and his descendants?

_____

_____

_____

4. Isn't it interesting that God chose an Iraqi (specifically, a Chaldean) named Abram—who eventually became known as Abraham—and told him to uproot his entire household, travel across the epicenter, and settle in the land that would become known as Israel? Isn't it fascinating, too, that Abraham listened to God and obeyed without complaint? Could Abraham really have anticipated what the future held for him? Could he possibly have foreseen the full extent to which the Lord was going to bless his descendants? What thoughts or questions do these events stir in you?

_____

_____

_____

5. Would you uproot your family and move to another country if God were to speak to you?

_____

_____

_____

6. These chapters of Genesis reveal God's heart of love and compassion for the people of the epicenter. He has a plan for them. He wants to bless them, not curse them. He wants to lead them on a great adventure, if they will only listen to him and follow him with all their heart. How about you? Do you believe that God loves you and has a wonderful plan for your life? Why or why not? (If you are curious about how to begin a personal relationship with God, please turn to the last section of this study for more information.)

_____

_____

_____

_____

7. Take some time to pray for the Lord to reveal himself more clearly to you. Ask him to show you how much he loves you. Ask him to show you the plan and purpose he has for you and your family. Then take some time to pray for the people of Iraq, Syria, Israel, and the rest of the epicenter, that they would read the Bible for themselves, understand God's heart of love and plan for their lives, and obey him as Abraham did.

_____

_____

_____

_____

CHAPTER ONE:
PREDICTING THE FUTURE

"It was one thing to write a novel that opened with a kamikaze attack against America that essentially comes to pass. But until that moment, few people had been talking publicly about the possibility of going to war with Iraq. Except me."

// *EPICENTER*, PAGE 4

1. *Where were you when you heard the news about Pearl Harbor? Where were you when you heard that John F. Kennedy had been shot?* These were common questions asked by previous generations of Americans. One of the defining questions for Americans today is, Where were you on September 11, 2001? What were you doing when you heard the news of the terrorist attacks in New York, Washington, and Pennsylvania?

   _____

   _____

   _____

   _____

2. Did the events of that day alter your thinking about national security, the role of the United States on the world stage, and the situation in the Middle East? If so, explain. If you live in a country other than the U.S., how did 9/11 affect you and your perspective?

   _____

   _____

   _____

   _____

3. Is it possible, in your view, for human beings to accurately and consistently predict the future? What about God? Is he able to tell us the future? Why or why not?

_____

_____

_____

_____

4. Look up the following verses. What is the common message of these passages?

JEREMIAH 33:3 • DANIEL 2:20-22 • DANIEL 2:27-28

AMOS 3:7 • 2 PETER 1:20-21

_____

_____

_____

_____

5. Do you believe the prophecies found in the Bible truly foretell future events, particularly specific events in specific epicenter countries? Why or why not?

_____

_____

_____

_____

6. Read the following Scriptures and note what each one says about God's Word:

    2 SAMUEL 22:31 • PSALM 119:16 • 2 TIMOTHY 3:16

_____

_____

_____

_____

7. Based on these Scriptures, what do we know about the credibility of biblical prophecy?

_____

_____

_____

_____

8. Of some 1,000 prophecies found in the Bible, scholars say that half of them have already come true. The rest deal specifically with events that will happen in history's last days, in the millennial kingdom, and beyond. What are some examples of Bible prophecies that have already come true?

_____

_____

_____

_____

CHAPTER TWO: THE GENESIS OF JIHAD

"As I sat with Natan Sharansky on that flight to New York in the fall of 2000, I tried to connect the dots. Never before in human history had Russia and Iran been allies. But according to [Dr. Tim] LaHaye, Scripture said it would be in the last days. Was it possible that such an alliance was now beginning to form?"

// *EPICENTER*, PAGE 26

1. In Arabic, the term *jihad* can refer simply to the struggle against sin and wrongdoing within a person's soul. But this is not how men like Osama bin Laden and other Islamic extremists use the term. How do they define *jihad*? What do they say are their ultimate goals?

   _____

   _____

   _____

   _____

2. The vast majority of the world's 1.2 billion Muslims have no desire to wage war against the West or Israel or to annihilate Judeo-Christian civilization as we know it. However, a small but highly dangerous number of Islamic extremists do. Why? What do you think drives that hatred?

   _____

   _____

   _____

   _____

3. How serious, in your opinion, is the threat of radical Islamic jihadists? What are some of the worst-case scenarios?

_____

_____

_____

_____

4. What are some of the reasons, in your view, that it has been so hard to make peace between the Israelis and Palestinians? Are you optimistic about the future? Why or why not?

_____

_____

_____

_____

5. In the late 1990s, Benjamin Netanyahu and Natan Sharansky were growing concerned that Russian nuclear warheads and Russian nuclear scientists could fall into the hands of radical Arab and Islamic regimes in the Middle East, namely the mullahs of Iran or Saddam Hussein's Republic of Iraq. Do you think they were right to be concerned? Why or why not?

_____

_____

_____

6. What were the circumstances that brought Joel Rosenberg and Natan Sharansky together? What was the ultimate outcome of their meeting? Has God ever brought someone into your life who was an unwitting catalyst for you?

_____

_____

_____

_____

7. Do you know any Jewish people who believe that Jesus is the Messiah? How did they come to that conclusion? How has it changed their lives?

_____

_____

_____

_____

CHAPTER THREE:
CONNECTING THE DOTS

*"It struck me that the scenario arising out of Ezekiel 38 and 39
actually wasn't bad: What if a dictator rose to power in Russia,
formed a military alliance—a nuclear alliance—with Iran,
and tried to attack Israel and seize control of the oil-rich Middle
East? . . . How might Bush respond? How might an Israeli prime
minister like Netanyahu or Sharon respond?"*

// *EPICENTER*, PAGE 38

1. What, if any, were your impressions of the situation in the Middle
   East back in 2000 when the Camp David Summit collapsed without
   a deal, Ariel Sharon visited the Temple Mount, and Yasser Arafat
   unleashed a new round of horrific violence? Do you remember
   Osama bin Laden's al Qaeda terrorists attacking the USS *Cole*? or
   Saddam Hussein threatening to invade Israel? Did you think the
   U.S. or other Western powers were likely to be engaged in mul-
   tiple wars in the region before long?

   _____

2. Do you agree that evangelical Christians are "among Israel's most
   loyal and steadfast friends" (*Epicenter*, p. 35)? Why or why not?

   _____

3. Given Genesis 12:1-3, in which God says he will bless those who bless the descendants of Abraham—and thus the children of Israel—how should followers of Jesus treat Jews in general and Israel in particular?

_____

_____

_____

4. Does this mean we should ignore the rights and needs and aspirations of the Palestinian people, or the Egyptians, or the Jordanians, or the Syrians, or the Lebanese?

_____

_____

_____

5. How should followers of Jesus approach the Arab-Israeli conflict?

_____

_____

_____

6. Historically, what has been the relationship between Egypt and Israel? How did that relationship change in 1979?

_____

_____

_____

7. Why do you think Egypt is not mentioned in Ezekiel 38 or 39?

_____

_____

_____

8. Historically, what has been the relationship between Iraq and Israel? How did that relationship change in 2003?

_____

_____

_____

_____

9. Why do you think Iraq (known in the Bible as Babylon, Mesopotamia, Chaldea, or Shinar) is not mentioned in Ezekiel 38 or 39?

_____

_____

_____

10. Do you think it is prophetically significant that we are living in the first window in human history in which Egypt and Iraq are not poised to be directly involved in the next major regional war with Israel? Why or why not?

_____

_____

_____

11. Have you ever read something in God's Word that didn't seem to make sense at the time but later made perfect sense? What does this tell you about God's reliability?

_____

_____

_____

_____

SETTING THE
STAGE: PART I

Starting on page 26 of *Epicenter*, the author describes how intrigued
he was with the prophecies of Ezekiel and the idea that a Russian-
Iranian alliance would form against Israel in the "last days." But what
first struck him was the notion that Ezekiel 36–37 and several related
prophecies had already come true—in his lifetime.

Before looking at the prophecies of Ezekiel 38 and 39 concerning the War of Gog and Magog, let's set the stage. Let's examine several key Bible prophecies whose fulfillment will precede this coming
apocalyptic war, and let us try to truly understand what they mean and
whether they have already come to pass.

PROPHECY: THE DESTRUCTION OF JERUSALEM

To begin, did the ancient Hebrew prophets really tell us that Jerusalem would be destroyed, the Holy Temple would be demolished,
and the Jewish people would be driven out of the Holy Land? Or,
to be more precise, did the Bible predict the events of the Roman
destruction of Jerusalem in AD 70 and the dispersion of the Jewish
people for nearly the next nineteen centuries? Consider the evidence
for yourself.

Read Daniel 9:24-26. There is an enormous amount of material
here worth considering in great depth, more than we can do justice to
right now. For our purposes, let's simply consider the order of events
that Daniel tells us would happen someday.

- First, Daniel 9:25 tells us that a decree will be issued to rebuild Jerusalem after the Babylonian destruction. (Note: Daniel was originally exiled from Jerusalem to Babylon by the forces of King Nebuchadnezzar. See Daniel chapter 1.)
- Second, Daniel 9:25 tells us that a long period of time will ensue in which Jerusalem is rebuilt, even though this will happen during "times of distress."
- Third, Daniel 9:26 tells us that when Jerusalem is rebuilt, the Messiah will come and then be "cut off."
- Fourth, Daniel 9:26 tells us that once the Messiah is cut off, the city of Jerusalem and the sanctuary (that is, the Temple) will be destroyed.

These four elements of Daniel's prophecy have already been fulfilled in history.

- In Nehemiah 2:1-8, we read the account of Persian King Artaxerxes issuing the decree to rebuild Jerusalem. (Note: Daniel wrote his prophecy around 530 BC. Artaxerxes issued the decree in 444 BC. Nehemiah then wrote his account around 430 BC.)
- Nehemiah began rebuilding Jerusalem as soon as he arrived in the city after Artaxerxes empowered him to go. He encountered stiff opposition from Israel's neighbors. Wars raged on and off in the region over the next several hundred years as the reconstruction and improvements continued. King Herod continued improving upon the city and dramatically expanded and enlarged the Second Temple, beginning around 19 BC.
- Jesus of Nazareth was born around the turn of the millennium. Scholars say he was crucified—or "cut off" from Jewish society—sometime between AD 30 and AD 33.
- Jerusalem and the Temple were destroyed and the Jewish people scattered in AD 70.

1. Read Matthew 23:37-39. What does Jesus say is going to happen to the city of Jerusalem in light of the city's rejection of his love and compassion?

_____

_____

_____

_____

2. Read Matthew 24:1-2. Just after describing the fate of Jerusalem, what did Jesus say would happen to the Second Temple?

_____

_____

_____

_____

PROPHECY: THE REBIRTH OF ISRAEL

As predicted by the ancient Hebrew prophets and Jesus himself, Jerusalem and the Second Temple were destroyed. But did the prophets really say that Israel would eventually be resurrected as a nation in the "last days" of human history? Let's consider the evidence.

1. Read Ezekiel 37, what Bible scholars call the "Vision of the Valley of Dry Bones." Look specifically at verse 11. What nation does the prophet say the dead, dry, scattered bones represent?

_____

_____

_____

2. How does this chapter describe the feeling of the Jewish people at the time? Are they hopeful or optimistic about their chances for survival? for rebuilding their nation in the promised land? Do they

seem to believe God is with them and will keep his promises to them? How do you think this compares to how the Jewish people felt during the Russian pogroms and the Nazi Holocaust?

_____

_____

_____

_____

3. Read Ezekiel 37:12-13. Despite the feelings of the Jewish people, what does God, through the ancient prophet, promise to do? What did happen in the early part of the 1900s, specifically in 1948, and since?

_____

_____

_____

_____

4. Beginning on November 2, 1917, with the British adoption of the famed Balfour Declaration, the modern State of Israel began a lengthy process of rebirth. The Balfour Declaration stated:

> *"Dear Lord Rothschild, I have much pleasure in conveying to you, on behalf of His Majesty's Government, the following declaration of sympathy with Jewish Zionist aspirations which has been submitted to, and approved by, the Cabinet: 'His Majesty's Government view with favour the establishment in Palestine of a national home for the Jewish people, and will use their best endeavours to facilitate the achievement of this object, it being clearly understood that nothing shall be done which may prejudice the civil and religious rights of existing non-Jewish com-*

munities in Palestine, or the rights and political status enjoyed by Jews in any other country.' I should be grateful if you would bring this declaration to the knowledge of the Zionist Federation. Yours sincerely, Arthur James Balfour."

With this in mind, read Ezekiel 37:5-8. Does the prophet say Israel will be reborn—indeed, resurrected—instantly, or through a process? In what ways is Ezekiel's prophecy an accurate picture of what happened in Israel in 1917 and afterward?

_____

_____

_____

_____

5. Are you old enough to remember David Ben Gurion declaring the official rebirth of the State of Israel on May 14, 1948? Was that significant to you at the time? If you weren't old enough, talk to some people who were, particularly Jews and devout Christians. What were their impressions? Did they ever imagine they would see such Bible prophecies come true in their lifetime?

_____

_____

_____

_____

CHAPTER FOUR:
THE THIRD LENS

"How could people so smart, so well versed in ancient and modern history, and so well informed by the best classified intelligence money can buy have so badly misread the situation?"
// *EPICENTER*, PAGE 46

1. American political and military leaders said they never imagined that anything like the terrorist attacks of 9/11 could happen in the United States. What's your view? Was 9/11 a failure of intelligence, a failure of imagination, or both?

_____

_____

_____

_____

2. Why do you think Washington was blindsided by the Iraqi invasion of Kuwait in 1990 and the events of 9/11? Why were American leaders blindsided by Auschwitz, Dachau, and Pearl Harbor?

_____

_____

_____

_____

3. "Too many in Washington today have a modern, Western, secular mind-set that either discounts—or outright dismisses—the fact that evil is a real and active force in history" (*Epicenter*, pp. 46–47).

Read the following passages and consider what they say about the nature of evil:

GENESIS 6:5 • JOB 34:10 • PSALM 5:4 • EZEKIEL 33:11

_____

_____

_____

_____

4. What do you think accounts for the reluctance of many world leaders to admit the reality of evil? How might the world be different if the existence of evil were acknowledged by those in power?

_____

_____

_____

_____

5. In looking at world events, the two most common "lenses" are the political and economic. What is the "third lens"? What are some of the ways you currently use the third lens in evaluating events in the Middle East and around the world?

_____

_____

_____

_____

6. Dangerous times require great wisdom and discernment. Read 1 Chronicles 12:32. Why does the Bible speak so highly of the "sons of Issachar"? What made them unique and special?

_____

_____

_____

7. Read the words of Jesus in Luke 12:54-56. What is the point of this passage? Was Jesus really criticizing his followers for wanting to know the weather forecast? What specifically did he want his followers to be doing and thinking about? In what ways does Jesus want his followers to be like the sons of Issachar?

_____

_____

_____

8. Do you agree with the following statements? Why or why not?

   Events such as the rebirth of the State of Israel, wars and instability in the Middle East, recent earthquakes, and the 2004 tsunami in Asia are evidence that we are living in what the Bible calls the last days.

   The rebirth of the State of Israel in 1948 and the return of millions of Jews to the Holy Land after centuries of exile represent the fulfillment of Biblical prophecies.

_____

_____

_____

CHAPTER FIVE:
FUTURE HEADLINE: ISRAEL DISCOVERS MASSIVE RESERVES OF OIL, GAS

"Israel has made extraordinary—some would say miraculous—economic gains since 1948 and has become dramatically wealthier than any of its immediate neighbors."
// *EPICENTER*, PAGE 64

1. Review the following passages. What do these verses say about the prosperity of Israel in the last days?
   EZEKIEL 36:11 • DEUTERONOMY 33:13-16 • ISAIAH 51:3

   _____

   _____

   _____

2. What specific promises are made to Israel in the following passages?
   GENESIS 49:25 • DEUTERONOMY 33:13 • ISAIAH 45:3

   _____

   _____

   _____

3. According to the author, what resources are meant by the phrases "the deep lying beneath," "the treasures of darkness," and "hidden wealth of secret places"? Do you agree with that assessment?

   _____

   _____

_____

_____

4. Why does it seem illogical through the "first and second lenses" that Israel would have access to these resources?

_____

_____

_____

_____

5. Discuss the recent evidence that, indeed, such resources _may_ be available in Israel after all. According to the chapter and from your own analysis, what prophetic significance might such discoveries hold for Israel and for the rest of the world?

_____

_____

_____

_____

CHAPTER SIX:
FUTURE HEADLINE: TREATIES AND TRUCES LEAVE ISRAELIS MORE SECURE THAN EVER BEFORE

"Looking through the third lens of Scripture, it is clear that the God of Israel is in charge, no matter what happens with Russia, Iran, Hamas, or other current or future enemies."

// *EPICENTER*, PAGE 69

1. Strife in the epicenter is a staple of the daily news feeds. What does the Bible tell us to expect in Matthew 24:6?

   _____

   _____

   _____

2. And yet, what does God say about the status of Israel in the following verses?

   EZEKIEL 38:8 • EZEKIEL 38:14

   _____

   _____

   _____

3. What specific developments in recent years did Major General Yaakov Amidror, the former head of assessment for Israeli Military Intelligence, point to suggesting that "Israel today is more strategically secure than at any other point since her birth" (*Epicenter*, p. 68)?

   _____

   _____

_____

_____

4. Do you agree or disagree with Shimon Peres that "there is no con-
tradiction between fighting terror and negotiating for peace" (*Epicenter*, p. 74)? Explain your viewpoint.

_____

_____

_____

5. What are the most recent developments in the Arab-Israeli peace
process? What are the signs of hope?

_____

_____

_____

_____

6. Conversely, what are some of the developments in recent years
that suggest another major war is coming to the epicenter?

_____

_____

_____

_____

SETTING THE STAGE: PART II

In an earlier study, we discovered that the predictions of the ancient Hebrew prophets concerning the destruction of Jerusalem and the Second Temple, the scattering of the Jewish people, and the rebirth of Israel have, in fact, come true. Now let's continue by examining three more key Bible prophecies whose fulfillment will precede the War of Gog and Magog. Some of the questions in this study may require a little additional research, but finding the answers will be worthwhile in evaluating whether these prophecies have truly been fulfilled.

PROPHECY: JEWS RETURN TO THE HOLY LAND

Did the ancient Hebrew prophets really say that Jews would return to the Holy Land after centuries of exile? Consider the following Bible prophecies.

EZEKIEL 36:10-12 • EZEKIEL 36:19, 23-24 • EZEKIEL 37:25-26
JEREMIAH 31:8

1. What are the specific promises God made through the ancient prophets to the exiled and scattered Jewish people?

_____

_____

_____

2. When did the Jewish people begin returning in significant numbers to the Holy Land after the Romans destroyed Jerusalem in AD
   70? What were some of the historic milestones in the twentieth-
   century return of the Jewish people to the land of Israel?

   _____

   _____

   _____

   _____

3. After the collapse of the Soviet Union on Christmas Day, 1991,
   how many Jews returned to the land of Israel? What percentage
   of Israelis are from Russia or the former Soviet Union? And why
   was the release of Jews from the USSR so significant historically?

   _____

   _____

   _____

   _____

PROPHECY: ISRAEL WILL MAKE THE DESERTS BLOOM

Did the ancient prophets really say the Jews would make the deserts
of the promised land bloom again in the end times? Consider the following Bible prophecies:

   EZEKIEL 36:8-9 • EZEKIEL 36:30 • EZEKIEL 36:35 • ISAIAH 27:6

1. What are the specific promises God makes to the Jewish people
   concerning the physical land of Israel?

   _____

   _____

_____

_____

2. What was the condition of the land of Palestine (the common
   name at that time) before 1948? Was it fruitful? Was it lush, green,
   or fertile?

_____

_____

_____

_____

_____

3. What is the condition of the land of Israel today? What made the
   difference? Hard work of the Jewish immigrants was a huge fac-
   tor, to be sure. What role do you think God played? Is this, in your
   view, the fulfillment of Bible prophecy?

_____

_____

_____

_____

PROPHECY: ISRAEL WILL REBUILD
THE ANCIENT RUINS

Did the prophets say that the Jews would rebuild the ancient ruins of
the promised land in the end times? Consider the following passages:

EZEKIEL 36:10 • EZEKIEL 36:33 • JEREMIAH 30:18, 24

1. What specific promises does God make to the Jewish people concerning the rebuilding of the ancient ruins of Israel?

_____

_____

_____

_____

2. Do some research on the building boom that has been under way in Israel over the last century or so. When did the boom begin? What are the trends? What has been the status of housing prices in Jerusalem, for example, in recent years?

_____

_____

_____

_____

3. Have you had the opportunity to visit Israel? Have you ever visited Jerusalem, Nazareth, Bethlehem, or Jericho? They once were in ruins, but today they are completely rebuilt and functional cities. What does this tell us about the reliability of Bible prophecy?

_____

_____

_____

_____

CHAPTER SEVEN:
FUTURE HEADLINE: A CZAR RISES IN RUSSIA, RAISING FEARS OF A NEW COLD WAR

"How could I be so certain that one day the world would see head-lines announcing that a dictator has risen to power in Russia, is rebuilding the Russian military, and is drafting a plan to conquer the Middle Easy and destroy Israel?"

// EPICENTER, PAGE 82

We are now ready to examine the prophecies of Ezekiel 38–39 in detail. Let's begin by defining "Gog." It is not a personal name. We are not looking for the rise of a "Dmitri Gog" or an "Ahmed Gog" or a "Fred Gog." Rather, it is a title, like a pharaoh or a czar. So who is he? What will he do? How will we know when he has emerged?

1. Read Ezekiel 38:1-3. What does this passage tell us about Gog?

   - What is his role?
   - Where is he from?
   - What territories does he rule over?
   - What is his relationship with God?

   _____

   _____

   _____

   _____

2. Read Ezekiel 38:10. What kind of plan will this political leader develop? What does this tell us about his character and intentions?

   _____

   _____

_____

_____

3. Read Ezekiel 38:4, 7, and 9. Is Gog a man of peace? Why or why not?

_____

_____

_____

4. Look carefully at Ezekiel 38:2-7. Gog will also be an international leader, capable of assembling a vast coalition. How many different nations are represented in the alliance Ezekiel describes?

_____

_____

_____

_____

5. Examine Ezekiel 38:8. What country will Gog specifically target?

_____

_____

_____

6. Read the following passages. What are the geographic clues Ezekiel provides? Where will this coalition that Gog will lead against Israel come from?

EZEKIEL 38:6 • EZEKIEL 38:15 • EZEKIEL 39:2

_____

_____

_____

_____

7. Review the map on page 83 of *Epicenter*. What modern countries are in the geographic location that Ezekiel suggests, vis-à-vis Israel?

_____

_____

_____

8. In addition to the geographic clues in the text, why do many Bible scholars believe that Gog is a political and military leader from Russia? What guidance, for example, does the Roman historian Josephus provide? (See *Epicenter*, pp. 82–87.)

_____

_____

_____

9. By no means do all Bible scholars agree that Magog is Russia or that Gog is a Russian political and military dictator. What do you think?

_____

_____

_____

_____

10. Why is Vladimir Putin increasingly perceived as a "rising czar"? What are some actions he is taking at home and abroad that cause concern among Western leaders and in Israel?

_____

_____

_____

_____

11. Given what Scripture tells us about Gog, do you think it is possible that Putin or someone close to him has the potential to be the ruler prophesied in Ezekiel 38? Why or why not?

_____

_____

_____

_____

CHAPTER EIGHT:
FUTURE HEADLINE: KREMLIN JOINS "AXIS OF EVIL," FORMS MILITARY ALLIANCE WITH IRAN

"When one looks at Russia through not only the political and economic lenses but also through the third lens of Scripture, one sees that Russia is, in fact, destined to become an enemy of the West, and particularly of Israel, in part because of its alliance with Iran."

// *EPICENTER*, PAGE 104

1. In Ezekiel 38:5, which is the first country named as part of the Russian alliance? What is this country called today? When did this name change occur?

_____

_____

_____

_____

2. Read Ezekiel 38:12. What will the invading alliance hope to achieve?

_____

_____

_____

3. For about 2,500 years after Ezekiel wrote this prophecy, Russia and Iran did not have a military or political alliance. Indeed, they had

great animosity toward one another. But since the late 1980s, that has been changing. Describe some of those changes given in *Epicenter* (pp. 104–110).

_____

_____

_____

_____

4. *Epicenter* was published in September 2006. What are some ways that Russia and Iran have accelerated their geopolitical alliance even further since then?

_____

_____

_____

_____

5. Prior to reading *Epicenter*, had you read Ezekiel 38–39? Had you ever heard of what Bible scholars call the War of Gog and Magog? Do you believe the emerging military and political alliance between Russia and Iran could be evidence of Bible prophecy coming true? Why or why not?

_____

_____

_____

_____

6. How dangerous for Israel are the prospects of Russia helping Iran become a nuclear power?

_____

_____

_____

7. Are there risks for Russia? for Iran? If so, what are they?

_____

_____

_____

8. What are the theological beliefs that seemed to be driving Iranian President Mahmoud Ahmadinejad after his election in June 2005? How does Ahmadinejad's eschatology differ from the teachings of Jesus Christ?

_____

_____

_____

9. What are some specific ways you can be praying for the leaders of Russia and Iran? Take some time to pray for them now.

_____

_____

_____

_____

CHAPTER NINE
FUTURE HEADLINE: MOSCOW EXTENDS MILITARY ALLIANCE TO INCLUDE ARAB, ISLAMIC WORLD

"While Iran is the first country identified as a future ally of Russia, there are others, and it is important that we identify them before we look to see if Russia is building military partnerships with such countries today."
    // *EPICENTER*, PAGE 128

1. Look up Ezekiel 38:5-6 and list the place names mentioned there.

    _____

    _____

    _____

2. Look at the chart on page 132 of *Epicenter*. Based on the sources cited on pages 128–132, what are some historical clues that these ancient names do, in fact, correspond to these modern countries?

    _____

    _____

    _____

3. Which of these countries have fought in wars against Israel in the past? What is the primary religion practiced in each of these countries, and how might those religious beliefs affect the nations' views of Israel?

    _____

    _____

_____

_____

4. How do we know that the following wars involving Israel (which have already taken place) do not qualify as the War of Gog and Magog?

ISRAEL'S WAR OF INDEPENDENCE IN 1948

THE SIX DAYS' WAR OF 1967

THE YOM KIPPUR WAR OF 1973

_____

_____

_____

5. Briefly describe some of the steps Russia has taken over the last decade or so to build alliances with the very countries that Ezekiel describes.

_____

_____

_____

6. It is striking that Russia is, in fact, building alliances with these Ezekiel countries. But let's be clear: this is not definitive proof that the War of Gog and Magog is going to happen in our lifetime, much less soon. Still, based on all that you have read in this study and on your own so far, do you think it is possible you will live to see these prophecies come to pass? Why or why not?

_____

_____

_____

_____

7. What are some ways that you can be praying for the people and the leaders of the Muslim world? Take some time to pray for them now.

_____

_____

_____

_____

USING THE THIRD LENS: PART I

To truly understand the tensions in the epicenter—past, present, and future—we must understand the spiritual roots of those tensions. That is, we must use the third lens to examine and answer four key questions:

- Who are the "chosen people," and why were they chosen?
- What is the "promised land," and who received the promise?
- What fuels the battle for the epicenter?
- Does God love and bless only the Jewish people?

We'll start by examining two of these questions in this study.

WHO ARE THE CHOSEN PEOPLE?

1. Read Genesis 18:17-19. To whom is the Lord speaking? For what purpose did the Lord choose him? From what did the Lord save him?

_____

_____

_____

2. Read Deuteronomy 7:6 and Deuteronomy 14:2. In both passages, to what people group is the Lord speaking? Why does the Lord say he has chosen them?

_____

_____

_____

_____

3. Read Deuteronomy 7:13-14. How does the Lord say he will treat these chosen people? How will these people be blessed in comparison to other people groups?

_____

_____

_____

_____

4. Read Deuteronomy 7:7-8. What does God say is *not* the reason he chose the children of Israel? What does he say *is* the reason?

_____

_____

_____

_____

5. Read Deuteronomy 9:4-6. What does the Lord warn the children of Israel not to think about themselves? How many times in this passage does the Lord warn the children of Israel on this subject?

How does the Lord describe the children of Israel from his perspective?

_____

_____

_____

_____

6. Read Leviticus 20:26. What expectation does the Lord have of the children of Israel? How does he plan to treat them in comparison to other people groups?

_____

_____

_____

_____

The Bible clearly says that the Lord did not choose the Jewish people because they were holy or righteous, nor because they were more numerous or more powerful than any other people group in the world. Why then did he choose them? The Lord of the universe chose them because he wants to demonstrate his supernatural desire and ability to love people and bless them and make them a blessing to others. He wants to teach the rest of mankind about his character through his relationship with the Jewish people. He wants to teach us that he cares for us and has a wonderful plan for our lives even if we are not great or powerful or righteous in and of ourselves; that he will keep his promises even when we occasionally break ours; that he will never leave or abandon us but loves us—as he says in Jeremiah 31:3–"with an everlasting love." Does this make you look at the Jewish people differently, knowing these Scriptures? Does it make you look at God differently?

WHAT IS THE PROMISED LAND?

In Genesis 15:18, the Lord says to Abram, "To your descendants I have given this land, from the river of Egypt as far as the great river, the river Euphrates." Pull out a map of the Middle East. Put one finger on the Nile River in Egypt. Put another finger on the Euphrates River in Iraq. That's an enormous tract of land, isn't it? The children of Israel have not yet governed all that territory in history. Many Bible scholars believe the true fulfillment of this promise will occur in the thousand-year reign of Jesus Christ as King of the entire earth, a period of time known as the millennial kingdom. That said, the Bible clarifies that the descendants of Abraham will, in fact, live in a smaller portion of this promised land, in the territory once known as "the land of Canaan."

1. Take a moment and read Genesis 17:8. To whom is the Lord speaking in this passage? How long will this person and his descendants own this land that has been promised to them?

   _____

   _____

   _____

   _____

2. Read Genesis 35:6-12. What does God Almighty promise to Jacob, as he promised to Abraham and Isaac before him? What new name does the Lord give to Jacob?

   _____

   _____

   _____

   _____

3. Read Genesis 48:3-4. What does Jacob tell his son Joseph? How long will Jacob and his descendants be allowed to possess the land of Canaan?

_____

_____

_____

_____

4. Read Genesis 50:24. What does Joseph, then living in Egypt, tell his brothers about who owns the land of Canaan?

_____

_____

_____

5. Read Exodus 12:25. What does Moses, speaking in the context of the Passover rituals, say about who owns the land of Canaan and why?

_____

_____

_____

6. Read Exodus 33:1. What country are the children of Israel living in when the Lord speaks to Moses? To what land does the Lord send

the children of Israel? To what three men and their descendants does the Lord say the land belongs?

_____

_____

_____

_____

7. Read Deuteronomy 11:10-12. According to these Scriptures, how does the Lord feel about the "promised" land, the land of Israel?

_____

_____

_____

_____

8. Take some time to read through Joshua chapters 14 through 20. Also note Joshua 21:43 and 45, which read: "So the Lord gave Israel all the land which He had sworn to give to their fathers, and they possessed it and lived in it. . . . Not one of the good promises which the Lord had made to the house of Israel failed; all came to pass." What do we learn about God's character from these passages? Does he simply make promises, or can he be trusted to keep them too?

_____

_____

_____

_____

9. We learn through these early books of the Bible that the God of Israel is a promise-making and a promise-keeping God—not just to the Jews living thousands of years ago but to us today as well. But we also learn in the Bible that while the Lord did promise the land of Israel to the Jewish people as an "everlasting possession," he created some conditions. Consider the following passages of Scripture. What are the benefits to the Jewish people of obeying the Lord? What is the price for severe, consistent, willful disobedience to the Lord?

    DEUTERONOMY 28:1-2 • DEUTERONOMY 28:15, 25, 64

    _____

    _____

    _____

    _____

10. There is a heavy price that the Lord says the children of Israel will pay if they turn their hearts away from him and act corruptly. But what about the Lord's covenant with Abraham to give the land of Israel to the Jewish people as an "everlasting possession"? *Everlasting* means forever, doesn't it? This means that the Jews *own* the land forever, but they are not always entitled to *live* in the land. The gift of the land by God to the Jews was an *unconditional promise*. The right to stay in the land and be blessed there, on the other hand, was a *conditional promise*. Is this the case that you find in the Scriptures? If not, what verses would you cite to make the case that the gift of the land to the Jews was a conditional promise that could be revoked?

    _____

    _____

    _____

11. Read Nehemiah 1:7-9. What happens if the Jewish people turn their hearts back to the Lord? Is it too late for them to return to the land of Israel? Or does the Bible suggest that God is a God of second chances, and third chances, and so forth?

_____

_____

_____

_____

12. Now consider some other passages. Of all the cities on the planet, which one does the Lord say He has chosen for Himself, according to the Bible?

    1 KINGS 11:32 • 2 CHRONICLES 6:6 • PSALM 132:13-14
    ZECHARIAH 3:2

_____

_____

_____

_____

13. In summary, is it fair to say that based on these and other passages of Scripture, God has chosen the Jewish people, the land of Israel, and the city of Jerusalem for himself, to shape and bless and guide as he sees fit? What are the implications of such truths?

_____

_____

_____

CHAPTER TEN:
FUTURE HEADLINE: GLOBAL TENSIONS SOAR AS RUSSIA TARGETS ISRAEL

"While it may be tempting to believe that the Russian Bear is dead and buried and poses no threat to Israel, the U.S., or anyone else, Ezekiel makes it clear that the Bear is only hibernating and will soon be back with a vengeance."

// EPICENTER, PAGES 139–140

1. Israeli Prime Minister Ehud Olmert said in the spring of 2006 that "Russian President Putin emphasized several times [in his call with Olmert] that Russia would not take any step directed against Israeli interests and would not harm Israel's security" (*Epicenter*, p. 139). Do you agree with Olmert's assessment? Why or why not?

_____

_____

_____

_____

2. Consider the following verses. What do they tell us about the Russian-Iranian alliance's plans for Israel?
   EZEKIEL 38:8 • EZEKIEL 38:15-16 • EZEKIEL 39:2

_____

_____

_____

_____

3. Why do you think that so many world leaders risk being blind-sided when Russia and its allies attack Israel?

_____

_____

_____

4. Review the author's meeting with Vladimir Zhirinovsky on pages 142–145 of *Epicenter*. What is your reaction to this story, especially to what Zhirinovsky told Rosenberg and his father?

_____

_____

_____

_____

5. What did Israel discover about Russian intentions when it attacked PLO terrorists in Lebanon in 1982?

_____

_____

_____

_____

6. What do previously classified U.S. government documents tell us about Russian intentions toward Israel during the 1973 war?

_____

_____

7. What does the latest research tell us about Russian intentions toward Israel during the 1967 war?

_____

_____

_____

_____

8. Why, in your view, did more than one million Jews flee after the collapse of the Soviet Union and emigrate to Israel?

_____

_____

_____

_____

9. Based on your study of recent headlines, what are the latest Russian moves in the Middle East? Is Russia taking steps to protect Israel's safety or potentially putting Israel in danger?

_____

_____

_____

_____

CHAPTER ELEVEN:
FUTURE HEADLINE: NEW WAR ERUPTS IN MIDDLE EAST AS EARTHQUAKES, PANDEMICS HIT EUROPE, AFRICA, ASIA

"It is entirely consistent with God's character and his plan and purpose throughout history for him to use times of judgment against some to shake up—and wake up—others to their need for a personal relationship with him."

// *EPICENTER*, PAGE 168

1. Let's go back to Genesis 12:1-3. Based on these verses from the Bible, what risks are Russian leaders taking by aligning themselves with those who hate and curse Israel and the Jewish people?

   _____

   _____

   _____

   _____

2. How did Adolf Hitler and Joseph Stalin choose to express their anti-Jewish sentiments in the twentieth century? What happened to them and their countries?

   _____

   _____

   _____

   _____

   _____

3. What Middle East leader seems to be carrying on in the anti-Semitic spirit of Hitler and Stalin? What are his declared intentions toward Israel? Is he, in your view, a real threat to Israel or just a big talker?

_____

_____

_____

4. Where in Ezekiel 38 does the Bible list *Israel's* allies in the last days? Who will come to Israel's aid?

_____

_____

_____

5. Take a moment to read Judges 16:28-30. What, then, is the "Samson Option," and how might Israeli leaders use the Samson Option in the face of a genocidal threat to the Jewish state?

_____

_____

_____

_____

6. In what specific ways will God judge the enemies of Israel, according to Ezekiel 38:18-23?

_____

_____

_____

_____

7. What will be the aftermath of the War of Gog and Magog? List the *physical* consequences found in these verses:

EZEKIEL 39:4-5 • EZEKIEL 39:9-12

_____

_____

_____

_____

8. Now read Ezekiel 39:22-24. What will be the *spiritual* consequences of the War of Gog and Magog? How will God use the war for his purposes?

_____

_____

_____

9. Read Ezekiel 39:21 and meditate on it for a while. Will only Israel be blessed? What will Israel's neighbors see? What will the world see? What could be some of the ripple effects of the War of Gog and Magog?

_____

_____

_____

_____

10. Given the human suffering and tremendous devastation that will occur, is this a time in history to which we should be looking forward? How would God want followers of Jesus Christ to respond when these events take place?

_____

_____

_____

_____

CHAPTER TWELVE:
FUTURE HEADLINE: IRAQ EMERGES FROM CHAOS AS REGION'S WEALTHIEST COUNTRY

"Those who argue that Iraq's liberation will not succeed in bringing about a season of stability and prosperity are making the mistake of viewing current events through only political and economic lenses. . . . For when one views Iraq's future through the third lens of Scripture, a much different picture emerges."
// *EPICENTER*, PAGES 172–173

1. What are the hoped-for outcomes of the current war in Iraq?

_____

_____

_____

_____

2. Why do you think so many Western political leaders have held little hope for the future of Iraq?

_____

_____

_____

3. According to the evidence presented in *Epicenter*, what signs of Iraq's religious, economic, military, and political freedom are already starting to appear?

_____

_____

_____

_____

4. Since *Epicenter* was published, what has been happening in Iraq? Has there been any progress in stopping the sectarian violence? If so, how much? What are the elements behind such progress?

_____

_____

_____

_____

5. Are you hopeful that the Iraqi people will be living in peace and prosperity in the next five to ten years? Are you more hopeful than you were a few months or years ago? Why or why not?

_____

_____

_____

_____

6. The Bible makes it clear that Babylon (Iraq) will undergo God's judgment for being a wicked city (Revelation 18). But before that happens, describe what Iraq the country and Babylon the city will be like, based on the following verses:

REVELATION 18:9-12 • REVELATION 18:14-16 • REVELATION 18:22

_____

_____

_____

_____

7. Will Iraq's wealth save it from ultimate destruction, based on its wickedness? What does this tell you about the importance of worldly wealth and prosperity in God's economy?

_____

_____

_____

_____

8. What are some specific ways that you can be praying for the people and leaders of Iraq? Take some time to pray for them now.

_____

_____

_____

_____

USING THE THIRD LENS: PART II

We have seen that according to the Bible, the Lord has chosen the Jewish people for his own. He has said he loves the Jewish people. He says he wants to bless them. He says he wants to set them apart and make them holy. He has also promised to give them the land of Israel as an "everlasting possession."

But none of this is happening in a vacuum, is it? What, then, fuels the battle for control of the people and land of the epicenter? And how does God feel about the other people groups of the world? In this study, we'll continue our examination of the four questions critical to gaining a biblical understanding of what is driving the people and events of the ancient and modern Middle East.

WHAT FUELS THE BATTLE FOR THE EPICENTER?

According to the Bible, Satan—also known in Scripture as the devil and Lucifer—is fundamentally and completely opposed to God and his divine purposes. What, then, can we assume Satan's approach toward the State of Israel and the Jewish people might have been throughout history? Since the Bible teaches us that God has chosen the Jewish people to bless them, does it not stand to reason that Satan has chosen them to curse them? Since God has promised to give the Jewish people the land of Israel, does it not stand to reason that Satan has vowed to steal it away? Since God has chosen to make Jerusalem the "city of peace," doesn't it make sense that Satan seeks to make it a city of bloodshed? Let's examine some Scriptures on this subject.

1. Read John 10:10. Jesus describes himself as coming to give mankind an abundant life. What does Jesus say are the general goals of Satan, whom he describes as a thief, toward mankind?

_____

_____

_____

_____

2. Read the first half of 1 Chronicles 21:1. What does this verse tell us about Satan's approach toward the land and people of Israel?

_____

_____

_____

_____

3. Read 2 Corinthians 2:11. The apostle Paul teaches us not to be ignorant of Satan's schemes. What might some of those schemes be with regards to Israel and the Jewish people?

_____

_____

_____

_____

4. Who are some of the geopolitical leaders and organizations in the news today trying to destroy the Jewish people, radically and violently divide or take all of the land of Israel, or violently divide or seize Jerusalem for themselves and their causes?

_____

_____

_____

_____

5. Read Jeremiah 31:35-37. In this passage, what does God say would have to happen before he would allow the Jewish people to be utterly destroyed? What would have to happen before God completely rejected the Jewish people and the nation of Israel in particular for their sins and mistakes?

_____

_____

_____

_____

6. Based on this passage, do you think either or both of these scenarios are likely to happen? Why or why not?

_____

_____

_____

_____

DOES GOD LOVE AND BLESS
ONLY THE JEWISH PEOPLE?

The Bible clearly teaches that the battle for the epicenter is ultimately a supernatural battle between God and Satan. Those who curse Israel and the Jewish people and seek to destroy them are in grave danger of triggering God's judgment and response.

But let us be crystal clear: the Scriptures also teach that God loves and want to bless Israel's neighbors. He won't bless those who curse Israel (see Genesis 12:1-3), but the Bible is clear that God does want to bless those who want to live beside Israel in peace and security. He also stands ready to bless those who turn away from hatred and violence and want to follow him and bless his chosen people.

Let's consider some specific passages.

1. Read Psalm 145:9. According to this verse, is God good to only some people? Does God restrict his mercies?

_____

_____

_____

_____

2. Turn to Isaiah 49:5-6. When the Messiah comes, what people group does the Lord (through the prophet Isaiah) say will be blessed first? Will God restrict his blessing to that group? What other nations will see the Messiah's light? How far will God's message of salvation reach?

_____

_____

_____

_____

3. Read John 3:16. According to this passage, how many people on the earth does God love? Is God's love and everlasting life restricted to just Jews? just Gentiles?

_____

_____

_____

4. Read Matthew 4:23-25. According to this passage, does Jesus bless only the Jewish people living in Galilee and going to the synagogues? To what other countries does the news of Jesus' love and compassion spread? How does Jesus respond to the people coming from those countries?

_____

_____

_____

5. To better understand the specific dynamic driving the Arab-Israeli conflict, take some time to read Genesis chapters 12 through 22. In these passages, God promises to bless Abram and Sarai, make them a great nation, give them a unique land, and bless them with a special son through whom "all the families of the earth will be blessed." (Gen. 12:3). Note, however, that Abram loses faith at one point and has a son with Sarai's Egyptian maid. Consider three key passages. What is the name of the son Abram has with Hagar? What kind of boy will this be? What kind of relationship will this boy have with those around him? Will God bless Abram's first son? How so?

GENESIS 16:11-12 • GENESIS 17:20 • GENESIS 21:17-18

_____

_____

_____

_____

6. Now focus on Genesis chapters 22 and 26. Who is the son God originally promised to Abraham? Which son does the Bible say Abraham nearly sacrifices? How does God react to Abraham's willingness to do whatever he asked of him? Through whose lineage—Isaac's or Ishmael's—does the Lord say that "all the nations of the earth shall be blessed"?

GENESIS 22:15-18 • GENESIS 26:24

_____

_____

_____

_____

7. Based on your reading of these passages, does God love both Ishmael and Isaac? Does God promise to bless both? Does God have a plan for both? Do you think God is justified or unfair to have a different plan and purpose for Ishmael's life than for Isaac's?

_____

_____

_____

_____

8. Isaac and Ishmael and their descendants are brothers. According to the following passages, how are brothers supposed to treat each other? How does Jesus teach his followers to treat their neighbors? How does Jesus say we are to treat our enemies?

ROMANS 12:10 • LEVITICUS 19:18 • MARK 12:28-31
GALATIANS 5:14-15 • MATTHEW 5:42-45

_____

_____

_____

_____

9. Given thousands of years of violence and bloodshed perpetrated by both sides of the Arab-Israeli conflict, is it even possible to love Israel *and* her neighbors *and* her enemies? How? Where do we get the power to love those who may not love us and may even hate us?

_____

_____

_____

_____

10. Before beginning this *Epicenter* study, had you ever prayed for the nation of Israel? Had you ever prayed for Israel's neighbors and her enemies? What are some specific and practical ways you could pray for the descendants of Isaac and the descendants of Ishmael, who are locked in what at times seems an interminable conflict? What are the names of the leaders on both sides of the conflict? What are specific ways you can pray for each of them?

_____

_____

_____

CHAPTER THIRTEEN: FUTURE HEADLINE: JEWS BUILD THIRD TEMPLE IN JERUSALEM

"The Temple Mount is the most dangerous square mile on the planet."
// *EPICENTER*, PAGE 191

1. Do you believe that one day there will once again be a Jewish Temple standing on the Temple Mount in Jerusalem? Why or why not?

   _____

   _____

   _____

   _____

2. Read through Ezekiel 40–48. What comes after the War of Gog and Magog?

   _____

   _____

   _____

3. What other evidence do we have that there will be a Temple in Jerusalem in the last days? Consider the following passages:

   ISAIAH 2:2 • ISAIAH 56:7 • MICAH 4:1 • DANIEL 9:27
   MATTHEW 24:15 • HAGGAI 2:6-9 • EZEKIEL 37:26-28
   EZEKIEL 40–48 • 2 THESSALONIANS 2:4 • REVELATION 11:1, 19

   _____

   _____

_____

_____

4. How will this come about? The Bible doesn't tell us. It just says that the Temple will, in fact, be there. What, then, do you envision the future Temple to be like?

_____

_____

_____

_____

5. What religious shrines currently stand on the Temple Mount? What would be the likely reaction if Jews tried to remove those buildings to erect the Third Temple?

_____

_____

_____

_____

6. Read Numbers 19:2, 9. What is the significance of the red heifer? What recent related event was an encouraging sign for the Jewish people?

_____

_____

_____

7. Do you believe the Temple treasures might be hidden somewhere by God for safekeeping? If so, do you believe he will eventually allow these treasures to be found and put into the last days Temple? Why or why not? Read the following verses. What clues, if any, do these passages give us?

JEREMIAH 27:21-22 • ISAIAH 52:11 • 2 CHRONICLES 35:3

_____

_____

_____

_____

8. Read the following passages. What is true treasure? How hard should we seek it?

PSALM 119:11-12 • PROVERBS 2:3-5

_____

_____

_____

_____

CHAPTER FOURTEEN:
FUTURE HEADLINE: MUSLIMS TURN
TO CHRIST IN RECORD NUMBERS

"How big is your God?"
// *EPICENTER*, PAGE 223

1. In Matthew 16:18, Jesus said: "I will build my church; and the gates
   of hell shall not prevail against it" (KJV). What forces, organizations, and governments are currently trying to prevail against the
   church in the epicenter?

   _____

   _____

   _____

2. What evidence is there today that Jesus Christ is, in fact, building
   and growing and strengthening his church despite intense spiritual, political, and violent radical opposition? In what countries is
   the growth happening the biggest and the fastest?

   _____

   _____

   _____

3. What are the main ways Muslims in the epicenter are hearing
   about the gospel of Jesus Christ?

   _____

   _____

   _____

4. Explain how recent Muslim conversions to Christianity seem to be fulfilling prophecy found in Acts 2:17-20 and Joel 2:28-31.

_____

_____

_____

5. Review the story of Farahat on pages 206–207 of *Epicenter*. How does his story illustrate the following Scriptures? What does this teach us about God's love for all of the people of the epicenter?
   MATTHEW 5:3 • I CORINTHIANS 4:13

_____

_____

_____

_____

6. Read Jeremiah 49:34-39. What does this prophecy say will eventually happen to the government of Iran (Elam)? What is God's attitude toward the "king and princes" of Iran? Do you believe this passage could be connected to Ezekiel 38–39? Why or why not?

_____

_____

_____

7. Where in the previous passage does the Lord say he is going to move his throne? Given how quickly Christianity is growing in

Iran already, what might the future hold spiritually for the people of Iran after the fulfillment of this prophecy?

_____

_____

_____

_____

8. Read Daniel chapter 3. In what ways are the events inside Iraq today similar to the story of Shadrach, Meshach, and Abednego?

_____

_____

_____

_____

9. Review the experience of Brother Andrew as he preached the gospel to an audience of Hamas leaders (*Epicenter*, p. 222). What stood out to you about this story? How has it impacted the way you think about our "sworn enemies" and how we should approach them with the love of Jesus Christ? If God can and will open doors for followers of Jesus to take the gospel even to radical Islamic terrorists, are there any doors he will not open for those who truly want to serve him?

_____

_____

_____

_____

10. Do you have Muslim neighbors, relatives, or coworkers? How are you showing them the love of Christ and sharing the gospel with them? Do you pray for them? Are you struggling with resentment toward them, or fear, or even racism? Take some time now to talk with your Father in heaven. Confess any sinful feelings toward Muslims. Ask God to give you a heart of love and compassion. Ask God to show you how you can love your Muslim neighbors (and your Jewish neighbors, too, for that matter) in real and practical ways.

_____

_____

_____

_____

CHAPTER FIFTEEN:
TRACKING THE TREMORS

*"I realize there are many skeptics reading this book, people who are
certain all this is a fairy tale, not something to be taken seriously.
As I stated in the introduction, I am not trying to persuade you that
these events are going to happen. I am simply trying to explain what
the Bible says will happen, why it matters, and how it will change
your world."*

// *EPICENTER*, PAGE 229

1. What can the devastation of Hurricane Katrina teach us about the
range of human responses to warnings of coming disaster? Why
did so many people ignore the storm warnings? Why didn't the
mayor and governor do more to explain to people just how powerful the storm was going to be?

_____

_____

_____

2. Interestingly enough, in Ezekiel 38:9, we read that the War of Gog
and Magog will "come like a storm" against Israel. In what ways
was National Weather Service forecaster Robert Ricks playing a
role similar to that of the Hebrew prophet Ezekiel? Though Ricks
could not have stopped the hurricane from coming, what if he
hadn't issued dire, specific warnings of what was coming?

_____

_____

_____

_____

3. Why do you believe God chooses to warn us through Bible prophecies of certain threats that are coming in the future?

_____

_____

_____

4. What obligation, if any, do we have to study these threats, understand them, and explain them to others? What responsibility do we bear if we say nothing?

_____

_____

_____

5. Review the story of Esther (Esther 1–10). Though there are many differences between the War of Gog and Magog and the situation Esther faced, there are some similarities. The Jewish people in Esther's day were in grave danger and there seemed to be little immediate hope of survival. Yet just when all hope looked lost, something changed. God intervened quite dramatically. Consider specifically the situation at hand in Esther 4. What was Esther being asked to do? What were the dangers involved? What did Mordecai tell Esther her obligation was (verse 14)?

_____

_____

_____

_____

6. Take a look at Ezekiel 38:7. Note that God tells Gog to "be prepared" for the War of Gog and Magog. Think about that for a
   moment. If the God of the universe actually tells the chief enemy
   of Israel to get ready and be prepared for a major war in the epicenter, what ought the follower of Jesus Christ be doing?

   _____

   _____

   _____

   _____

7. Regardless of whether the War of Gog and Magog will happen
   soon, or even in our lifetime, what are some specific, practical
   ways that Christians can bless the nation of Israel right now? Consider the implications of the following verses:

   PSALM 122:6 • ISAIAH 61:1 • ISAIAH 61:4
   DEUTERONOMY 15:11

   _____

   _____

   _____

8. We dare not forget that the Bible teaches us that God loves Israel's
   neighbors and her enemies—and he commands us to love them
   too. What, then, are some specific, practical ways that we can love
   the Palestinians, the Lebanese, the Jordanians, the Syrians, the
   Egyptians, the Iraqis, the Sudanese, the Iranians, and so forth?

   _____

   _____

_____

_____

9. Read John 3:16 and John 14:6. Read also Revelation 3:20. Then read through the section in *Epicenter* on having an "exit strategy" (pp. 236–239.) Do you have a personal exit strategy? Have you asked Jesus Christ to be your personal Savior and the Lord of your life? If not, you can pray right now the same kind of prayer that Leonard Rosenberg prayed back in 1973:

> *Lord Jesus, I need you. Thank you for dying on the cross for my sins. Thank you for rising again from the dead to prove that you are the one you say you are, the only way to heaven. I open the door of my life and receive you as my Savior and Lord. Thank you for forgiving my sins and giving me eternal life. Take control of the throne of my life. Make me the kind of person you want me to be. In Jesus' name I pray, amen.*

_____

_____

_____

10. Did you just ask Jesus Christ into your life by faith in his death and resurrection? If so, welcome to the family of God! He has just adopted you and you have eternal life. Consider these two key verses. What does the Bible say about those who believe in the name of Jesus? How much confidence does the Bible say you can now have that you are going to heaven for eternity?

    JOHN 1:12 • I JOHN 5:13

_____

_____

_____

11. Read through the *Epicenter* section on having a "neighborhood strategy" (pp. 240–241). Do you have one? If not, as you have been going through this study, what has God been stirring in your heart for you to do with what you have learned? Review the list of suggestions in *Epicenter*. Would any of those ideas be helpful for you?

_____

_____

_____

_____

12. Take a moment now to read through the *Epicenter* section on having a "global strategy" (pp. 241–244). Do you have a global strategy? If you do, how can you be faithful in executing it and encouraging others to join you? If you don't, what are some ways you can "help others understand what is coming and know God's love and plan for the people who live in the epicenter" (*Epicenter*, p. 241)?

_____

_____

_____

_____

13. If you don't have a global strategy, would you consider joining the team at The Joshua Fund? This is a nonprofit educational and charitable organization designed "to bless Israel and her neighbors in the name of Jesus, according to Genesis 12:1-3." In 2008, The Joshua Fund launched "Operation Epicenter," a strategy to mobilize at least 100,000 Christians around the world to pray knowledgeably and faithfully for the peace of Jerusalem and for the needy people of the epicenter and to move $120 million worth of humanitarian relief supplies into Israel and the Muslim world

working in partnership with government leaders, hospitals, social service agencies, and local Christians in each country. Visit the Web site at www.joshuafund.net to find out more about the fund and its relief projects. You will also discover how every believer who is interested in caring for the people of the epicenter can "learn, pray, give and go."

---

14. Are you interested in making a financial contribution to the work of The Joshua Fund? The Joshua Fund has been established as an organization described in Section 501(c)(3) of the Internal Revenue Code, contributions to which are tax deductible for federal income tax purposes. The Joshua Fund limits administrative costs to only 10 percent of the budget, allowing a full ninety cents of every dollar of the resources you invest to go directly into projects that bless Israel and her neighbors. Most organizations of this nature devote between 15 and 30 percent for administrative costs. Please make your check payable to *The Joshua Fund* and send to:

THE JOSHUA FUND
18950 BASE CAMP ROAD
MONUMENT, COLORADO 80132-8009

---

14. As you come to the end of this study of the epicenter, what are some of the most intriguing things you have learned? What are some of the unresolved questions you still have? Do you have any

new, personal goals stemming from the Scriptures you have studied? If so, what are they and how do you plan to achieve these goals in the coming year?

_____

_____

_____

_____

CLOSING PERSONAL NOTE

I hope this Epicenter Study
Guide *has been helpful to you.
I am grateful for your interest
in this important subject, and
I pray that the Lord will richly
bless you and your family as
you bless Israel and her neighbors in the name of Jesus.*

Joel C. Rosenberg

PRAYER JOURNAL

PRAYER REQUESTS FOR THE EPICENTER   ANSWERS TO PRAYER

_____   _____

_____   _____

_____   _____

_____   _____

_____   _____

_____   _____

_____   _____

_____   _____

_____   _____

_____   _____

_____   _____

PRAYER REQUESTS FOR THE EPICENTER	ANSWERS TO PRAYER
_____	_____
_____	_____
_____	_____
_____	_____
_____	_____
_____	_____
_____	_____
_____	_____
_____	_____
_____	_____
_____	_____
_____	_____
_____	_____
_____	_____
_____	_____
_____	_____
_____	_____

APPENDIX: BIBLE PROPHECY AND YOUR SPIRITUAL JOURNEY

The number-one question I am asked as I travel around the world is, "How can you be Jewish and believe in Jesus?" I have been asked by reporters and talk radio hosts. I have been asked by members of Congress, generals, and diplomats. I was recently asked by an Islamic leader in the Middle East. It is an excellent question, and one that I am honored to answer.

Let's begin by considering a few important passages.

In Luke 2:25-35, an Israelite named Simeon blessed Jesus and told Mary, "Behold, this child is appointed for the fall and rise of many in Israel, and for a sign to be opposed—and a sword will pierce even your own soul—to the end that thoughts from many hearts may be revealed."

Anna, the Hebrew prophetess—and a widow at the age of 84—never left the Temple, continually fasting and praying. In Luke 2:36-38, we read: "At that very moment she came up and began giving thanks to God, and continued to speak of Him to all those who were looking for the redemption of Jerusalem."

In Acts 17:2-3, we read that the apostle Paul—a highly trained Jewish legal scholar—went into synagogues and "reasoned with them from the Scriptures, explaining and giving evidence that the [Messiah] had to suffer and rise again from the dead, and saying, 'This Jesus whom I am proclaiming to you is the [Messiah].'"

How did Simeon and Anna know Jesus was the Messiah?

Why were they so expectant that the Messiah was about to arrive?

How was Paul able to use the Scriptures to prove to the Jewish people that Jesus is the Messiah?

The fact is, the Hebrew Scriptures were filled with critical clues to the identity of the coming Messiah, clues I wholeheartedly believe were fulfilled by Jesus of Nazareth. On pages 261–267 of *Epicenter*, I describe my own spiritual journey at some length. But here, let me share with you a series of Scriptures that were helpful to me and my family as we came to believe that Jesus really is the Jewish Messiah and the Savior of the entire world. It is my prayer that as you study these Scriptures for yourself, they will be helpful to you as well.

Messiah will be born in Bethlehem.
MICAH 5:2-5A • (MATTHEW 2:5-6)

Messiah will be born of a virgin.
ISAIAH 7:14 • (MATTHEW 1:18-25)

Messiah will live and minister in Galilee.
ISAIAH 9:1-3 • (MATTHEW 4:12-16)

Messiah will teach with parables.
PSALM 78:2 • (MATTHEW 13:34-35)

Messiah will be a human child, a son, but be called "Mighty God" and "Prince of Peace."
ISAIAH 9:6 • (MATTHEW 27:54, EPHESIANS 2:14-18)

Messiah will have the "Spirit of the Lord" and bring "good news to the afflicted" and "proclaim liberty to the captives."
ISAIAH 61:1-3 • (LUKE 4:18-21)

Messiah will be "despised and forsaken."
ISAIAH 53:3, PSALM 22:1 • (MATTHEW 27:46)

Messiah will be betrayed by a friend.
PSALM 41:9 • (MATTHEW 26:23-25)

Messiah will be sold for thirty pieces of silver.
ZECHARIAH 11:12-13 • (MATTHEW 27:2-4)

Messiah will be mocked and sneered at.
    PSALM 22:6-8 • (MATTHEW 27:29)

Messiah will be surrounded by evil men who will pierce his hands and feet.
    PSALM 22:16, ZECHARIAH 12:10 • (MATTHEW 27:27-35, JOHN 19:34-38)

Messiah's enemies will cast lots for his clothes.
    PSALM 22:18 • (MATTHEW 27:35, JOHN 19:23-24)

Messiah will be tortured and killed "for our transgressions . . . crushed for our iniquities."
    ISAIAH 53:5 • (ROMANS 4:24-25)

Messiah will be a "guilt offering."
    ISAIAH 53:10 • (HEBREWS 10:10)

Messiah will be assigned a rich man's grave.
    ISAIAH 53:9 • (MATTHEW 27:57-60)

Messiah will live again.
    ISAIAH 53:10, PSALM 16:8-11 • (MATTHEW 28:1-20, ACTS 2:22-32)

Messiah will be cut off before Jerusalem is destroyed.
    DANIEL 9:27 • (MATTHEW 23:37-39 AND 24:1-2)

One last thought in this regard.

Many people ask me how I can believe that God has a son, aside from whether Jesus is, in fact, God's "only begotten Son," as John 3:16 tells us he is. Actually, it's not hard at all for me to believe that God has a son. I don't pretend to fully understand it. I cannot fully explain it. But the Hebrew Scriptures are crystal clear that the Lord God of Israel has a son and that we should honor him, get to know his name, and understand the price he has paid to cleanse us from our sins. Consider the following verses:

- Psalm 2:7, 10-12—"I will surely tell of the decree of the LORD: He said to Me, 'You are My Son, Today I have begotten You. . . . Now therefore, O kings, show discernment; Take warning, O judges of the earth. Worship the LORD with reverence and rejoice with trembling. Do homage to [or "Kiss"] the Son, that

He not become angry, and you perish in the way, for His wrath may soon be kindled. How blessed are all who take refuge in Him!"

- Proverbs 30:4—"Who has ascended into heaven and descended? Who has gathered the wind in His fists? Who has wrapped the waters in His garment? Who has established all the ends of the earth? What is His name or His son's name? Surely you know!"
- Zechariah 12:10—When the "Spirit of grace" is poured out on the Jewish people, "they will look on Me whom them have pierced; and they will mourn for Him, as one mourns for an only son, and they will weep bitterly over Him like the bitter weeping over a firstborn."

What do these passages mean?
What do they mean to you?

I want to thank the following people:

My dear wife, Lynn,
    God's greatest gift to me, aside from salvation itself;
Caleb, Jacob, Jonah, and Noah,
    may you become men of great courage and men committed to God's Word;
My parents, Leonard and Mary Rosenberg,
    for your sacrificial love and prayers;
June Meyers,
    who blessed me with her daughter and so much more;
Dr. T. E. Koshy and Dr. Indira Koshy,
    who helped me truly understand what it means to teach the Word and make disciples of all nations;
Edward Hunt and John Black,
    two dear brothers and colleagues who are now teaching the Word of God to a new generation of disciple-makers;
The Joshua Fund staff and board of directors,
    for loving the people of the epicenter enough to devote your lives to serving them;
Scott Miller,
    for being a great agent and friend;

Ron Beers, Becky Nesbitt, and the entire Tyndale House family,
who share my heart and my vision for writing books that change lives;
and Jennifer Leo,
for her kind assistance with an early draft of this study guide.

SUGGESTED READING

- *Are We Living in the End Times?* by Dr. Tim LaHaye and Jerry B. Jenkins

- *The Popular Bible Prophecy Commentary: Understanding the Meaning of Every Prophetic Passage* by Dr. Tim LaHaye and Ed Hindson

- *The Complete Book of Bible Prophecy* by Mark Hitchcock

- *The Second Coming of Babylon* by Mark Hitchcock

- *Every Prophecy of the Bible: Clear Explanations for Uncertain Times* by John F. Walvoord

- *The Final Act: Setting the Stage of the End Times Drama* by Chuck Smith

- *God's Blueprint for Bible Prophecy: Daniel* by Kay Arthur

- *Bible Prophecy for Kids: Revelation 1–7* by Kay Arthur and Janna Arndt

- *The Temple and Bible Prophecy: A Definitive Look at Its Past, Present, and Future* by Randall Price

- *Things To Come: A Study in Biblical Eschatology* by Dr. J. Dwight Pentecost

- *The Rise of Babylon* by Charles H. Dyer

- *Josephus: The Complete Works* by Flavius Josephus

- *Standing With Israel: Why Christians Support the Jewish State* by David Brog

- *Light Force: A Stirring Account of the Church Caught in the Middle East Crossfire* by Brother Andrew and Al Janssen

- *Secret Believers* by Brother Andrew and Al Janssen

- *Back To Jerusalem: Three Chinese House Church Leaders Share Their Vision to Complete the Great Commission* by Brother Yun, Peter Xu Yongze, Enoch Wang, with Paul Hattaway

FOR MORE INFORMATION:

www.joelrosenberg.com
www.joshuafund.net

And be sure to sign up for >> FLASH TRAFFIC <<,
Joel's free e-mail alerts and prayer updates at
www.joelrosenberg.com.

"Rosenberg has become one of the most **entertaining** and **thought-provoking** novelists of our day. Regardless of your political views, you've got to read his stuff."

>> RUSH LIMBAUGH

★ ★ ★

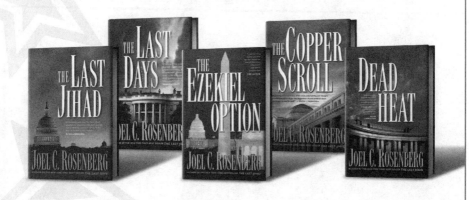

★ ★ ★

WWW.JOELROSENBERG.COM